Exploring English
GRAMMAR

D

Continental

Credits

Illustrations: Laurie Conley, Doris Ettlinger, Michael Fink, Estella Hickman, Margaret Lindmark, John Norton, Linda Pierce

ISBN 978-1-5240-0266-4

Copyright © 2017 The Continental Press, Inc.

Table of Contents

Introduction to
Exploring English Grammar

You use language every day to speak, listen, read, and write. Using language effectively helps you to communicate your thoughts and ideas to those around you. To understand and use the English language, you must understand and use the rules of grammar. Knowing parts of speech, punctuation, sentence structure, and capitalization rules helps you to master the English language. *Exploring English Grammar* reviews important language rules to help you grow into a skillful communicator.

Exploring English Grammar includes skills in the following areas:

- Sentence structure
- Nouns
- Verbs
- Verb tenses
- Pronouns
- Adjectives
- Adverbs
- Types of sentences
- Capitalization
- Punctuation
- Word usage
- Letter writing

UNIT 1: Sentences

Sentences and Fragments

Remember A **sentence** is a group of words that tells a complete thought. If the words do not tell a complete thought, they are a **fragment.**

Sentence Deer eat leaves and berries.

Fragment Eat leaves and berries.

Sentence Too many deer in one place can harm plants.

Fragment Too many deer in one place.

Think About Read the examples again. Look at both sentences. Then look at the fragments. What is the difference between them?

_____

_____

_____

Read and Apply Read each group of words. Write **S** above each sentence. Write **F** about each fragment.

Large packs of hungry wolves. Wolves often eat

deer. Yet wolves are not harmful to deer herds. Only the

sick and weak deer. Without wolves, deer herds would

become too large. Could not find enough leaves and

berries. Many deer would starve. Better off with wolves

around. These animal "enemies" actually help one

another. Wolves and deer.

Write About

Find each group of words that you marked **F** for fragment in Read and Apply. Add words to the group to make it a sentence that tells a complete thought. Write the complete sentences below.

_____

_____

_____

_____

_____

_____

_____

_____

_____

_____

Review

Listen to the group of words. Circle **SENTENCE** or **FRAGMENT** for each group of words you hear.

1. SENTENCE   FRAGMENT

2. SENTENCE   FRAGMENT

3. SENTENCE   FRAGMENT

4. SENTENCE   FRAGMENT

5. SENTENCE   FRAGMENT

6. SENTENCE   FRAGMENT

7

Subject

Remember   A sentence has two parts. The **subject** part tells who or what the sentence is about. The **simple subject** is the noun or pronoun that the sentence tells about. The **complete subject** is the main word and all the words that tell about it.

complete subject
↓
<u>Several different <u>plants</u> grow in deep water.</u>
↑
simple subject

Think About   What is the difference between the simple subject and the complete subject?

_____

_____

Read and Apply   Read the sentences. Underline the complete subject in each one. Circle the simple subject.

Many ponds are covered with water lilies. Their long, tough stalks grow up from the mud. Their round, flat leaves lie on the surface of the water. Many different insects sit on the leaves. The large, white blossoms can be one foot across.

These remarkable flowers are useful as well as beautiful. Their roots suck plant and animal wastes out of the water. A few plants can really clean up a dirty pond.

8

Write About   Write a paragraph about an interesting plant that you have seen. Then underline each complete subject in your paragraph. Circle each simple subject.

_____

_____

_____

_____

_____

_____

_____

_____

_____

_____

Review   Complete each sentence by adding a subject. Use the subjects in the box or think of your own. Circle the simple subject.

| Many people | Various types of fish |
| Interesting plants | A backyard pond |

1. _____ enjoy having ponds in their backyards.

2. _____ needs a pump to keep the water moving.

3. _____ do well in backyard ponds.

4. _____ can grow in and around ponds.

Predicate

Remember The **predicate** part of a sentence tells what the subject does or is. The **simple predicate** is the verb or verb phrase that tells what the subject does or is. The **complete predicate** is that main word or phrase and all the words that go with it.

simple predicate   complete predicate
↓   ↓

Artists use different types of materials to make art.

Some will make art with objects from nature.

Think About Is the simple predicate always just one word? Explain.

_____

_____

Read and Apply Read the sentences. Underline the complete predicate in each one. Circle the simple predicate.

Chakaia Booker is a sculptor. Her artwork is not made out of clay or stone. She creates detailed sculptures from old tires. Chakaia has been known to make art that she wears, too. She can use these pieces as clothing! Chakaia likes the different shades of black found in tires. They make her think of the different African American skin tones. Chakaia's sculptures can be seen in art galleries and parks.

Write About

Write a paragraph about a piece of art you have made. What did you use to make it? Then underline each complete predicate. Circle each simple predicate.

_____

_____

_____

_____

_____

_____

_____

_____

_____

_____

Review

Complete each sentence by adding a predicate. Use the predicates in the box or create your own. Circle the simple predicate.

> will research a piece of art
> enjoy collecting art from around the world
> came from people's collections
> may travel to other countries looking for a special piece

1. Some people _____.

2. They _____.

3. A collector _____.

4. Many pieces in museums _____.

11

Declarative and Interrogative Sentences

Remember   A **declarative sentence** tells about something. It ends with a **period (.).** An **interrogative sentence** asks about something. It ends with a **question mark (?).**

Interrogative   **Have you ever been lost in the woods?**

Declarative   **It is best to stay in one place until someone finds you.**

The word order is different in declarative and interrogative sentences.

The play will end by noon.
Will the play end by noon?

Question words *who, what, when,* and *where* can be used to make interrogative sentences.

When will the play end? What is the name of the play?

Think About   Look at the examples above. How do you know which are declarative sentences and which are interrogative sentences?

_____

_____

Read and Apply   Read the sentences. Write **D** above each declarative sentence. Write **I** above each interrogative sentence.

Who was Garrett Morgan? Why is he important? Garrett Morgan was

an inventor. Have you ever heard of a gas mask? This was one of Garrett's

inventions. He made a special hood. People could wear it to go into smoky

rooms. Garrett used it to rescue men trapped in a tunnel.

Did Garrett Morgan invent anything else? He invented a traffic signal.

Was his signal the first one ever made? No, but it did work better than

others. Soon cities around the country were using Garrett's design.

12

Write About

Change the word order to write the interrogative sentences as declarative sentences or to write the declarative sentences as interrogative sentences.

1. Did Garrett Morgan make a hair straightening product?

_____

2. Garrett would wear his special hood to show people how it worked.

_____

Use a question word to write an interrogative question based on the given sentence.

3. Garrett Morgan lived in Cleveland, Ohio.

_____

_____

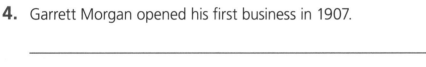

4. Garrett Morgan opened his first business in 1907.

_____

_____

5. Garrett Morgan had a shop to repair sewing machines and shoes.

_____

_____

Review

Listen to each sentence. Circle **DECLARATIVE** if it is a declarative sentence. Circle **INTERROGATIVE** if it is an interrogative sentence.

1.   DECLARATIVE   INTERROGATIVE

2.   DECLARATIVE   INTERROGATIVE

3.   DECLARATIVE   INTERROGATIVE

4.   DECLARATIVE   INTERROGATIVE

5.   DECLARATIVE   INTERROGATIVE

Exclamatory and Imperative Sentences

Remember

An **exclamatory sentence** shows surprise or strong feeling. It ends with an **exclamation point (!).**

What a fun time we had!
This tastes great!

An **imperative sentence** asks or tells someone to do something. It usually ends in a period. If it shows surprise or strong feeling, it ends with an exclamation point.

Rake the leaves into a pile.
Don't let them blow away!

Think About

Look at the imperative sentences. Do these sentences have a subject? If so, what is it?

_____

_____

Read and Apply

Read the sentences. Write **E** above each exclamatory sentence. Write **I** above each imperative sentence. Some sentences are not exclamatory or imperative.

What interesting creatures spiders are! They are helpful to

people. They eat harmful insects. Some spider venom, or poison,

can be used as medicine. Spiders can also be used as food!

Cooked tarantula is a popular dish in some countries. Use two adult

tarantulas. Remove the abdomen of the spider. Remove the hairs from the

legs of the spider. Coat the spider in batter and then fry it in oil. What a

treat! Would you like to try one?

Write About

Write a paragraph about a strange food you have heard of or eaten. Use at least one exclamatory sentence and one imperative sentence. Underline and label the exclamatory and imperative sentences.

_____

_____

_____

_____

_____

_____

_____

_____

_____

_____

Review

Listen to each sentence. Circle **EXCLAMATORY** if it is an exclamatory sentence. Circle **IMPERATIVE** if it is an imperative sentence.

1.   EXCLAMATORY   IMPERATIVE

2.   EXCLAMATORY   IMPERATIVE

3.   EXCLAMATORY   IMPERATIVE

4.   EXCLAMATORY   IMPERATIVE

5.   EXCLAMATORY   IMPERATIVE

15

Run-On Sentences

Remember   A sentence tells a complete thought. Two or more thoughts written together are not a sentence. They are a **run-on sentence.**

Run-on   How did women help during the American Revolution some followed their husbands in the army.

Sentences   How did women help during the American Revolution? Some followed their husbands in the army.

Think About   How do you show that a sentence is beginning? How do you show that a sentence is ending?

_____

_____

Read and Apply   Read the sentences. Use the proofreading marks on the right to correct any run-on sentences.

Mary Ludwig Hays received the nickname Molly Pitcher during the American Revolution the Battle of Monmouth happened in June 1778. It was very hot on the battlefield. Mary carried pitchers of water to the soldiers. Her husband was firing a cannon he fell over because of the heat. Mary took over at the cannon she helped to fight for the rest of the battle. When it was over, George Washington thanked Mary for her work.

≡   make a capital letter

⊙   add a period

16

Write About Read these run-on sentences. Write each one correctly.

1. Lydia Darragh lived in Philadelphia her house was used by British troops.

   _____

   _____

2. One night, the troops talked about their battle plans Lydia pretended to be asleep and listened.

   _____

   _____

3. Lydia wrote down the British troops' plans she took them to the American leaders.

   _____

   _____

4. The American troops were ready when the British attacked the British never figured out who told their plan to the Americans.

   _____

   _____

Review Read the sentences. Draw a line to show where to divide each run-on sentence into two sentences.

1. Some people say Molly Pitcher's story is not true she may not have been a real person.

2. Many women were spies during the American Revolution their stories were not all written down.

3. Today, we only know that women helped in many ways we will never know all of the things they did.

Compound Subjects

Remember   Sometimes two short sentences have the same predicate. Then the subjects can be joined by the word *and* to make a **compound subject.**

<u>Tortillas</u> are made with corn flour.

<u>Tamales</u> are made with corn flour.

Compound Subject   <u>Tortillas and tamales</u> are made with corn flour.

Think About   How is a compound subject different from a simple subject?

_____

_____

Read and Apply   Read the sentences. Underline the compound subjects. Circle the two sentences that could be combined by making a compound subject.

Fossils form in different ways. Amber and ice keep an animal exactly the way it was when it was alive. Mold fossils and cast fossils begin when an object creates a hollow shape in mud. A mold fossil shows the outside of the object. A cast fossil shows a copy of the object made out of minerals.

There are two types of fossils. Body fossils contain some part of an organism's body. Teeth are body fossils. Bones are body fossils. A trace fossil is something that an organism left behind. Footprints and burrows are trace fossils.

Write About Write a paragraph about things you have found in nature. Use at least one compound subject.

_____

_____

_____

_____

_____

_____

_____

_____

_____

Review Read each pair of sentences. Write them as one sentence with a compound subject.

1. Animals can turn into fossils. Plants can turn into fossils.

_____

_____

2. Insects have been preserved in amber. Dinosaur feathers have been preserved in amber.

_____

_____

3. Megalodons were prehistoric animals. Mammoths were prehistoric animals.

_____

_____

Compound Predicates

Remember Sometimes two short sentences have the same subject. Then the predicates can be joined by the word *and* to make a **compound predicate.**

A sailboat <u>tipped over.</u>

A sailboat <u>sank.</u>

Compound Predicate A sailboat <u>tipped over and sank.</u>

Think About How is a compound predicate different from a simple predicate?

_____

_____

Read and Apply Read the sentences. Underline the compound predicates. Circle the two sentences that could be combined by making a compound predicate.

Marco Polo explored and traveled to new places. Marco lived in Venice, Italy, and traveled to China. There he met Kublai Khan, the emperor of China. Kublai Khan liked Marco and made him a messenger. Marco traveled all over China. Marco learned to speak the language. After many years, Marco wanted to return to Italy. He wrote about his adventures and told stories about what he had seen.

Marco Polo

Write About   Write a paragraph telling what type of adventures Marco Polo might have had in China. Use at least one compound predicate.

_____

_____

_____

_____

_____

_____

_____

_____

_____

_____

Review   Read each pair of sentences. Write them as one sentence with a compound predicate.

1. Marco Polo lived in China for 17 years. Marco Polo wrote down the things he saw there.

_____

_____

2. Kublai Khan trusted Marco Polo. Kublai Khan asked his advice.

_____

_____

3. People read Marco Polo's book. People learned about places they had never seen.

_____

_____

Compound Sentences

Remember   Sometimes two short sentences can be joined by a **conjunction,** like *and, but,* or *or,* to make a **compound sentence.** *And* joins sentences that are about similar things. *But* joins sentences that tell about things that are different. *Or* joins sentences that give a choice between things.

Whales sometimes swim ashore, <u>and</u> no one knows why.

These mammals breathe air, <u>but</u> they cannot live on land.

They must be pulled out to sea, <u>or</u> they will die.

Think About   How many thoughts are there in a compound sentence?

_____

_____

Read and Apply   Read the sentences. Underline the compound sentences. Circle the two sentences that could be combined by making a compound sentence.

In the early 1800s, many Americans wanted to expand this country, but Native American tribes lived on the land they wanted. The American government said the tribes had to move. They sent soldiers to force the people to leave. The Cherokee people were told to leave their homes, or they would be killed. They had to travel thousands of miles. The journey was difficult, and many people died. This journey is now remembered as "The Trail of Tears."

Write About

Write a paragraph telling about a difficult decision you had to make. Use at least one compound sentence.

_____

_____

_____

_____

_____

_____

_____

_____

Review

Read each pair of sentences. Rewrite them as a compound sentence using the word *and, but,* or *or.*

1. Andrew Jackson was a soldier. He became president.

_____

_____

2. Many people voted against the Indian Removal Act. It still passed.

_____

_____

3. The Act said tribes had to leave their land peacefully. Soldiers would force them.

_____

_____

4. Andrew Jackson helped the country grow. He was cruel to Native American tribes.

_____

_____

UNIT 2: Nouns

Common and Proper Nouns

Remember A **noun** is a naming word. A **common noun** names any person, place, animal, or thing. A **proper noun** names a particular person, place, animal, or thing.

Common	singer	country	dog	day
Proper	Garth Brooks	China	Fido	Monday

Think About In what ways are common and proper nouns written differently?

_____

_____

Read and Apply Read the sentences. Underline each common noun. Circle each proper noun.

Angel Cordero Jr. was born in Puerto Rico. His father and uncle trained horses. Angel rode racehorses. He won many awards and races. He won the Kentucky Derby, Preakness Stakes, and Belmont Stakes. Those are the three biggest horse races in America. Angel won the Kentucky Derby three times. He won on Cannonade, Bold Forbes, and Spend A Buck. The jockey won many times at the racetrack in Saratoga. He said the best horse he ever rode was Seattle Slew.

A bad fall cut Angel's career short. He had 7,057 wins when he retired. Angel is a member of several special groups, including the National Museum of Racing and Hall of Fame.

Write About

Write a paragraph about a special award you have won or one you would like to win.

_____

_____

_____

_____

_____

_____

_____

Review

Listen to each noun. Circle **COMMON** if it is a common noun. Circle **PROPER** if it is a proper noun.

1.   COMMON   PROPER

2.   COMMON   PROPER

3.   COMMON   PROPER

4.   COMMON   PROPER

5.   COMMON   PROPER

Plural Forms

Remember A **singular noun** names one. A **plural noun** names more than one. To make most nouns plural, add *s* or *es*. If the noun ends in *y*, drop the *y* and add *ies*. If the noun ends in *f*, drop the *f* and add *ves*.

Singular	desk	church	pony	leaf
Plural	desk<u>s</u>	church<u>es</u>	pon<u>ies</u>	lea<u>ves</u>

Think About Look at the examples. What differences do you see between the singular and plural nouns?

_____

_____

Read and Apply Read the sentences. Underline each singular noun. Circle each plural noun.

Parchment is a special kind of paper. This material was made from the skin of goats and calves. First, hairs and fat were removed from the skins. Special knives were used to scrape the skin. Then, the hides were rubbed with stones. They were soaked in water and then stretched on a frame. Finally, they could be written on with brushes and ink.

26

Write About

Look at the words in the box. Write six sentences using the plural forms of these words. Use at least one of these words in each sentence. Do not repeat a word.

flower	beach	cherry	floor	puppy	scarf
shelf	family	fox	game	dish	city

1. _____

   _____

2. _____

   _____

3. _____

   _____

4. _____

   _____

5. _____

   _____

6. _____

   _____

Review

Read each noun. Choose the correct plural form.

1. **ferry**   A. ferrys   B. ferris   C. ferries   D. ferryes

2. **race**   A. races   B. racees   C. racies   D. raves

3. **bench**   A. benchies   B. benches   C. benchs   D. benchyes

4. **thief**   A. thiefes   B. thiefyes   C. thiefies   D. thieves

Irregular Plural Forms

Remember   Sometimes the plural form of a noun is a different word. Sometimes the singular and plural forms of a noun are the same word. These are irregular plural forms.

Singular	child	woman	foot	mouse	sheep	fish
Plural	children	women	feet	mice	sheep	fish

Think About   How can you remember irregular plural forms?

_____

_____

Read and Apply   Read the sentences. Put a line under the irregular plural forms of nouns. Use a dictionary if you need help.

The Wampanoag are a Native American tribe living in New England. At one time, they were farmers and hunters. The men hunted deer and small game, like quail and rabbits. They also caught fish from their canoes. The water was full of cod, bass, and flounder. The women grew corn, squash, and beans. They also gathered shellfish from the ocean and berries and nuts from the woods. When the Pilgrims arrived in America, the Wampanoag people helped them learn to survive in the New World.

Write About Write a sentence using the plural form of each noun. Use a dictionary if you need help.

1. tooth

_____

2. mouse

_____

3. sheep

_____

4. shrimp

_____

5. child

_____

Review Complete each sentence by writing the plural form of the given nouns on the lines. Use a dictionary if you need help.

1. We saw _____ and _____ at the pond.
　　　　　　　　goose　　　　　　　fish

2. Including antlers, _____ can grow to nine _____ tall.
　　　　　　　　　　　elk　　　　　　　　　　　　foot

3. Many _____ enjoy watching _____.
　　　　　person　　　　　　　　　wildlife

4. The _____ and _____ watched the play.
　　　　man　　　　　　　woman

29

Possessive Nouns

Remember A **possessive noun** names who or what has something. It shows ownership. Add *'s* to singular nouns and plural nouns that do not end in *s*. Add only an apostrophe to plural nouns that end in *s*.

Noun	friend	girls
Possessive Noun	friend's house	girls' books

Think About How are possessive nouns different from regular nouns?

_____

_____

Read and Apply Read the sentences. Underline each possessive noun.

     Animals' bodies are perfectly fitted for their uses. A duck's feathers keep out water. Beavers' tails are flat for slapping mud. A frog's skin is green so that the animal can hide in the grass. To protect them from cold weather, sheep's wool is thick. A snake's eyes have a covering to keep out dirt. People's bodies are also well designed. Just think of how many things a person's thumb does.

Write About Think of other animals you have seen. Write a paragraph telling how they are special.

_____

_____

_____

_____

_____

_____

_____

_____

_____

Review Complete each sentence. Fill in the blank with the possessive form of the given noun.

1. The _____ hats were on the bench.
        boys

2. _____ bike is in the backyard.
     Brittney

3. My _____ car is parked in the garage.
         parents

4. Carl put the _____ saddles in the barn.
              horses

5. The _____ sale starts tomorrow.
        store

6. Where is my _____ coat?
               sister

Abstract Nouns

Remember   An **abstract noun** names something that you cannot see, smell, taste, hear, or touch.

peace   belief   beauty   fact   idea

Think About   What is the difference between an abstract noun and other nouns?

_____

_____

Read and Apply   Read the sentences. Put a line under the abstract nouns. There are eight different abstract nouns.

Frederick Douglass was born into slavery. When he was young, a woman began to teach him to read. His master made her stop. He did not think slaves should have an education. Frederick had dreams of freedom. Finally, Frederick escaped. He spent the rest of his life fighting for the equality of all people. He told people the truth about the evils of slavery.

Write About

Write six sentences using abstract nouns. You may use the abstract nouns in the box or think of your own. Use at least one abstract noun in each sentence.

love	bravery	success	skill	peace
friendship	comfort	energy	memory	luck
patience	joy	talent	trust	happiness

1. _____

_____

2. _____

_____

3. _____

_____

4. _____

_____

5. _____

_____

6. _____

_____

Review

Listen to each noun. Circle **YES** if it is an abstract noun. Circle **NO** if it is not an abstract noun.

1.   YES   NO

2.   YES   NO

3.   YES   NO

4.   YES   NO

5.   YES   NO

UNIT 3: Verbs
Action Verbs

Remember   An **action verb** is a word that names an action. It tells what a noun does or did.

chop   grumbles   think   buzzed

Think About   Does a word have to name a movement to be an action verb? Explain your answer.

_____

_____

Read and Apply   Read the sentences. Underline each action verb.

A Greek legend tells how Jason searched for the Golden Fleece. This magic sheepskin hung on a tree in a faraway land. A fierce dragon guarded it. Jason sailed across the sea in his ship, the *Argo*. He took 50 men with him, and they met with many adventures. Jason almost died before he found the Golden Fleece. He stole it from the dragon. Princess Medea helped him. Then the dragon chased them, but at the very last minute they both escaped.

Write About   Write a paragraph about a time you looked and looked for something. Then circle each action verb in your sentences.

_____

_____

_____

_____

_____

_____

_____

_____

_____

Review   Complete each sentence by writing an action verb in the blank. Use the action verbs in the box or think of your own.

gives	lined	read	sit	buried

1. The dog _____ the bone in the backyard.

2. Our teacher never _____ homework on the weekend.

3. Brian _____ the word in the dictionary.

4. Please _____ in the chair by the window.

5. The class _____ up by the door.

Plain Form and s-Form Verbs

Remember The plain form of an action verb is used with a plural subject, which names more than one. The s-form of a verb is used with a singular subject, which names one. Make the s-form of a verb by adding *s* to the plain form. If the verb ends in *x, s, ch, sh,* or *o,* add *es* to the plain form. If it ends in a consonant plus *y,* change the *y* to *i* and add *es.*

Turtles <u>swim</u> in the water.

A turtle <u>lays</u> eggs.

It <u>goes</u> onto the beach.

It <u>dries</u> itself in the sun.

Think About How do you know which form of a verb to use?

_____

_____

Read and Apply Read the sentences. Find the five verbs that are in the wrong form. Put a line through each verb and write the correct form above it.

The blood in your body contains red and white blood cells.

Blood cells do important jobs. Red blood cells carries oxygen

through your body. They gets oxygen in the lungs. Then the

cells moves to the heart. The heart pumps blood to all parts

of the body. White blood cells fight disease. Sometimes your

body catch an infection. White blood cells finds the infection.

They destroy the infection to keep you healthy.

The Heart

Write About   Write a few sentences about another part of your body. Tell what it does. Be sure to use the correct forms of action verbs.

_____

_____

_____

_____

_____

_____

_____

_____

_____

Review   Complete each sentence by writing the correct form of the action verb on the line.

1. The cat _____ before sitting down.
             stretch

2. Katelyn and Matt _____ the dresser against the wall.
                        push

3. The dog _____ his owner.
               obey

4. Brent _____ to open the jar.
             try

5. The children _____ to the play area.
                    run

37

Linking Verbs

Remember   A **linking verb** connects the subject of the sentence to words in the predicate. It tells what the subject is or was.

am	was	become	seem
is	were	became	feel
are			

It <u>is</u> cold outside.

I <u>am</u> excited for snow!

Think About   Read the examples again. Which words do the linking verbs connect?

_____

_____

Read and Apply   Read the sentences. Underline each linking verb.

It was winter. People were sad. What was the problem? For a long time, doctors were no help. They seemed to not understand.

Now, scientists are ready with some answers. In winter, the days are shorter, and there is less sunlight. Without sunlight, some people become unhappy. As soon as summer is here, they feel better. The name for this is seasonal affective disorder.

38

Write About   Write a paragraph telling how you feel during the winter. Then circle each linking verb in your sentences.

_____

_____

_____

_____

_____

_____

_____

_____

_____

_____

Review   Circle the correct linking verb for each sentence.

1. I [am   is   are] in my bedroom.

2. Jeff and Jenny [was   were] excited.

3. The weather [become   became] colder.

4. The blanket [feel   feels] soft.

5. The students [seem   seems] ready for the test.

Helping Verbs

Remember   Sometimes a **helping verb** comes before the **main verb** in a sentence. It helps the main verb to tell about doing or being. Together, the two verbs are called a **verb phrase.**

helping verb ↓ ↓ main verb

These pine trees will be green all year.

Their needles have fallen a few at a time.

New ones are growing every day.

Some trees can reach 100 feet in height.

Think About   Read the examples again. Look at the verbs *will, have,* and *are.* Are these words always helping verbs?

_____

_____

Read and Apply   Read the sentences. Underline each verb phrase. Circle each helping verb.

For over 800 years, there have been llamas in Peru. A cousin of the camel, a llama will carry heavy loads. The llama has helped many people in the mountains. Now, campers are using llamas as pack animals. Sometimes angry llamas will spit at people. But usually a llama will be friendly. Many people are buying llamas as pets. They might use the wool to make products. Llamas can be work animals, too. The llama has found a new home in this country.

Write About   Write a paragraph telling about an unusual pet you have heard about or seen. Underline each helping verb and circle each main verb.

_____

_____

_____

_____

_____

_____

_____

_____

_____

_____

Review   Write helping verbs in the blanks to complete these sentences. Use a different helping verb in each sentence.

1. People _____ enter through either door.

2. Someone _____ eaten all of the bananas.

3. This flower _____ grow in shade.

4. Jasper _____ walk the dog tomorrow.

5. The girls _____ watching a movie.

Future Tense

Remember   The tense of a verb tells when the action happens. A verb in the **future tense** tells about something that is going to happen.

Main Verb   **take**

Future   Tomorrow, we <u>will take</u> a plane to Ireland.

Think About   Read the example again. What helping verb is used to make the future tense?

Read and Apply   Read the sentences. Underline the sentences that are in future tense.

Humans will live on Mars one day. Some people think so. They are making plans to send humans there. People will take all of the supplies they need with them. There will be nothing on Mars that they can use to survive. To make this happen, scientists will do a lot of research. Astronauts will go through training. They must learn to live in areas that are similar to Mars. This mission will not take place for many years. Maybe someday you will hear about the first people to reach Mars.

Write About Write a paragraph telling what you think it would be like to be one of the first people to live on Mars. Use future tense in your paragraph.

_____

_____

_____

_____

_____

_____

_____

_____

_____

Review Read the sentences. Rewrite each one with the helping verb *will* to make it tell about the future.

1. To live on Mars, people need food, water, and oxygen.

   _____

   _____

2. Special habitats protect them from the environment on Mars.

   _____

   _____

3. Satellites help them communicate with people on Earth.

   _____

   _____

43

Present Tense

Remember

A verb in the **present tense** tells about what is happening now or all the time. Its form changes to agree with the sentence subject. Just the verb is used with a plural subject and with the pronouns *you* or *I*. A suffix is added to the verb for a singular subject. Sometimes a change must be made in the root word when a suffix is added.

The teams <u>play</u> each Saturday. Our team <u>plays</u> well.

I <u>pitch</u> sometimes. Jodi <u>pitches</u> even better than I do.

We <u>try</u> to do our best. Everyone <u>tries</u> hard.

Think About

What suffixes are added to make verbs agree with singular subjects?

_____

_____

Read and Apply

Read the sentences. Find five verbs that are in the wrong form. Put a line through the verb and write the correct form above it.

Many people visits Notre-Dame Cathedral every day. A tour guide

teaches the visitors about the cathedral. This church stand beside the

River Seine in Paris, France. Ten bells hang in the two towers. Each tower

reachs 226 feet in the air. Round rose windows contain pieces of colored

glass. A stained-glass window catches the sun. The light makes beautiful

colors. Some visitors studies the statues on the church. Many statutes show

detailed features. No one hurrys through the cathedral. Each person tries to

respect this beautiful place.

44

Write About   Write a paragraph telling about a beautiful building you have seen or visited. Write your paragraph in present tense.

_____

_____

_____

_____

_____

_____

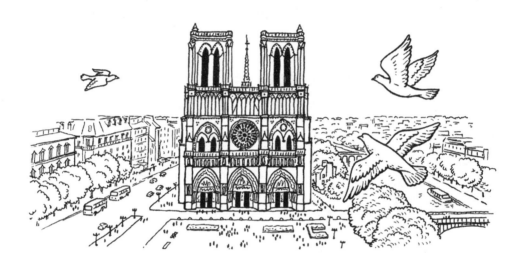

Review   Read the sentences. Write the correct form of the verb that is under each line.

1. A squirrel _____ an acorn in its mouth.
                   carry

2. Paul and Juan _____ the leaves.
                      rake

3. Mom _____ the car in the driveway.
             park

4. Kaylee _____ her doll's hair.
                brush

45

Past Tense

Remember   A verb in **past tense** tells about what has already happened. The past tense of most verbs is made by adding a suffix.

verb → **polish + ed = polished** ← past tense

rule + ed = ruled

Sometimes a change must be made in the root word when a suffix is added.

fry → fri + ed = fried   **dim → dimm + ed = dimmed**

Think About   Look at the examples. What happens to the root word of verbs that end in *e?* To verbs that end in a consonant plus *y?* To one-syllable verbs that end in consonant-vowel-consonant?

_____

_____

_____

Read and Apply   Read the sentences. Make the paragraph past tense by putting a line through each verb that needs to be changed. Write the past tense form above it.

For thousands of years, the people of Tahiti fish for food. Sometimes

the women wade into shallow water. Then they spear the fish swimming

there. The men usually sail out to sea every day. Each boat carry big nets.

The fishermen drop the nets into the ocean. Then they drag them slowly

through the water. They try to catch enough to feed their families. They also

hope to get a few extra. Then they trade the fish for other goods.

Write About   Write a paragraph telling about another way people got food in the past. Write your paragraph in past tense.

_____

_____

_____

_____

_____

_____

_____

_____

_____

_____

Review   Write the correct past tense form of each verb in the blank.

1. Mai _____ her fingers.
                snap

2. Tom _____ the history book.
              study

3. Mom _____ the table with a tablecloth.
              cover

4. Caleb _____ the last paper towel.
              use

5. Grandma _____ me on Tuesday.
              call

6. I _____ eggs on the stove.
              fry

47

 Lesson 8

Past Tense: Irregular Forms

Remember   The past tense of some verbs is made by changing their spelling or by making no change at all. For some, the word changes completely.

Present	make	go	see	grow	drive	give	become	put
Past	made	went	saw	grew	drove	gave	became	put

Think About   Read the examples again. How can you find out how a verb changes?

_____

_____

Read and Apply   Read the sentences. There are five verbs that are incorrect. Put a line through each incorrect verb. Write the correct form above it.

Alfred Nobel grow up in Sweden. He became wealthy by inventing

dynamite. It brought him millions of dollars. But Alfred see that his invention

could be harmful. People made dangerous weapons with it. Alfred knew he

did not want that. So he do something special. He write a will telling how

he wanted his money used when he died. He put his money in a special

fund. It go to start the Nobel Prize in science, literature, and peace.

Write About   Write a paragraph about something kind you did for another person. Write in the past tense.

_____

_____

_____

_____

_____

_____

_____

_____

Review   Read the sentences. Write the past tense of the verb that is under each line. Use the examples or a dictionary if you need help.

1. Dad _____ the car down the street.
        drive

2. Gisa _____ the book off the shelf.
        take

3. People _____ their bikes in the park.
        ride

4. The students _____ stars out of colored paper.
        cut

5. The teacher _____ his name on the board.
        write

6. We _____ our own vegetables.
        grow

Progressive Tense

Remember   **Progressive tense** uses a helping verb and the **present participle** of a verb. The present participle is made by adding *ing* to a verb.

Present Progressive
The bird <u>is</u> <u>flying</u>.

The men <u>are</u> <u>jogging</u>.

Past Progressive
The boys <u>were</u> <u>racing</u>.

The girl <u>was</u> <u>swimming</u>.

Think About   Look at the examples. What do you notice about how the verbs change when you add *-ing?*

_____

_____

Read and Apply   Read these sentences. There are five mistakes with helping verbs or present participles. Circle the incorrect words.

For years, people were killing sagebrush. Ranchers was burning it because their herds were refuseing to eat it. Companies were destroying it to make room for homes and oil fields. Now, scientists is trying to save this desert plant. The sage grouse is livving in the sage. Without it, these birds are disappearing. Now, people are working to protect the sage grouse. They is stopping the destruction of sagebrush. Their work is saving other animals, too.

Write About   Look back at the paragraph in Read and Apply. Rewrite the five sentences that have mistakes. Use the correct helping verb or present participle.

_____

_____

_____

_____

_____

_____

_____

Review   Listen to the sentences. Circle **YES** if the sentence is in progressive tense. Circle **NO** if it is not in progressive tense.

1.   YES   NO

2.   YES   NO

3.   YES   NO

4.   YES   NO

5.   YES   NO

51

Perfect Tense

Remember

Perfect tense uses the helping verbs *have, has,* and *had* and the **past participle** of the main verb. Some verbs have a special past form to use with *have, has,* and *had.*

Past Form	have worked	has saved	had hurried
Special Past Form	have gone	has taken	had drawn

Cynthia <u>threw</u> the javelin 150 feet. She <u>has thrown</u> well today.

Think About

Look at the special past form examples. What are the present and past tense forms of these verbs?

_____

_____

_____

Read and Apply

Read the sentences. Circle the verb that has a special past form.

People have competed in wrestling in the Summer Olympics since the first modern games. Men had taken part in wrestling matches in the ancient Olympic games, too. Women's competition has existed since 2004. Before the 2016 Olympics, the USA had never won a gold medal in women's wrestling. Helen Maroulis has changed that. At the end of the final match, Helen had defeated a three-time Olympic champion. Helen had earned the gold medal.

Write About Write five sentences in perfect tense. Use some of the verbs in the box. Do not use any verb twice. Use a dictionary if you do not know the past participle form of a verb.

rub	cut	find	give	fall	draw
get	buy	bring	ask	decide	stop

1. _____

   _____

2. _____

   _____

3. _____

   _____

4. _____

   _____

5. _____

   _____

Review Read the sentences. Write the correct past participle of the verb that is under each line.

1. Baseball games always have _____ a big crowd.
                                        draw

2. This group has _____ to protect endangered species.
                         try

3. The crossing guard had _____ the traffic.
                                 stop

4. We have _____ a lot of work on our house.
                   do

Pronouns

Remember A **pronoun** is a word that takes the place of a noun. A pronoun must agree with its **referent,** which is the noun it is replacing.

Peter put on his coat. It is bright green. He walked out the door. I stayed inside.

The pronoun *It* takes the place of the noun *coat.* The pronoun *He* takes the place of the noun *Peter.* The pronoun *I* does not have a referent.

Think About Think of other pronouns. Which pronouns can take the place of nouns that name people? Which can take the place of nouns that name animals, places, or things?

_____

_____

Read and Apply Read the sentences. Put a line under the pronouns. Circle the pronoun that does not agree with its referent.

Denali is the highest mountain in North America. Hudson Stuck and a group of climbers were the first to climb it. They reached the peak on June 7, 1913. In 1947, Barbara Washburn became the first woman to climb them. She climbed with her husband, Bradford. He had climbed it for the second time.

If you want to climb Denali, you must be prepared. You will need to plan and train for a year or more.

Write About

Write a paragraph telling about an adventure you have had or one you would like to have. Circle the pronouns that you use.

_____

_____

_____

_____

_____

_____

_____

_____

Review

Read the paragraph. Complete the sentences. Write a pronoun in each blank.

Mom and I visited a Hopi village. _____ was in the middle of the

desert. _____ spoke with some Hopi silversmiths. _____ make

beautiful jewelry. Mom bought a ring for _____. _____ also bought

a bracelet for my sister. My sister loved _____!

Subject and Object Pronouns

Remember   A **subject pronoun** takes the place of the subject part of a sentence. An **object pronoun** is used after an action verb and after a word like *to, of, by, with,* and *from.*

	Singular	Plural
Subject	I, you, he, she, it	we, you, they
Object	me, you, him, her, it	us, you, them

Think About   Read the examples again. Which object pronouns are also subject pronouns?

_____

_____

Read and Apply   Read the sentences. Put a line under the subject pronouns. Circle the object pronouns.

Have you heard of Elizabeth Blackwell? She was the first woman doctor in America. A friend encouraged her to go to medical school. Most schools would not accept her. They did not think a woman could be a doctor. Finally, she was accepted into a school. The students left her out at first. Soon she impressed them by working hard and doing well. Elizabeth graduated at the top of the class. We can thank Elizabeth Blackwell for opening the doors for other women doctors.

Write About Write six sentences. Use a subject pronoun in the first three sentences. Use an object pronoun in the last three sentences.

Subject Pronouns

1. _____

_____

2. _____

_____

3. _____

_____

Object Pronouns

4. _____

_____

5. _____

_____

6. _____

_____

Review Read the sentences below. Fill in the circle next to each sentence that uses a correct pronoun.

○ Him bought a new baseball cap.

○ They went to the park.

○ The girls asked her to play.

○ The teacher told they to sit down.

○ Us need to go home now.

○ Dad handed me a box of tissues.

57

Possessive Pronouns

Remember   A **possessive pronoun** tells who or what has something. It shows ownership.

Singular	my	your	his	her	its
Plural	our	your	their	

My parents bought their new car yesterday.

Think About   Which pronoun can be singular or plural?

Read and Apply   Read the sentences. Put a line under each possessive pronoun.

Most turtles have shells on the outside. Their shells give them protection. The Cantor's giant softshell turtle is different. Its ribs make a protective plate under its skin. This turtle gets its name from Theodore Edward Cantor. In his work as a reptile scientist, Cantor found and named this turtle.

The softshell turtle spends most of its life buried in the sand. Only its eyes and nose are above ground. The turtles surprise their prey. A female lays her eggs in February and March. Sadly, the Cantor's giant softshell turtle is now an endangered species.

Write About Tell about your relatives and where they are from. Circle the possessive pronouns you used.

_____

_____

_____

_____

_____

_____

_____

_____

_____

_____

Review Read the sentences. Write a possessive pronoun to complete each sentence.

1. We placed _____ lunches on the table.

2. Micah walks _____ dog every day.

3. Ava spilled water on _____ shirt.

4. _____ family had a picnic.

5. The horse stood in _____ stall.

Relative Pronouns

Remember A **relative pronoun** refers back to a noun earlier in the sentence. It introduces more information about the noun, or it identifies it.

Relative Pronouns who   whom   that   whose   which

The man <u>who</u> lost his umbrella ran to his car.

The house <u>that</u> is on the corner is for sale.

I spoke to the woman <u>whom</u> I saw at the store.

Think About What does a relative pronoun tell you about the information that comes after it?

_____

_____

Read and Apply Read the sentences. Put a line under each relative pronoun. Circle the noun that it refers to in the sentence.

Earth has a limited water supply that people can use. Many communities that are in third-world countries do not have access to clean water. People who live in these areas can get sick because they do not have clean water. Children who have to walk miles to fetch water are not able to go to school. Groups of people are trying to bring clean water to everyone. Organizations raise money, which helps to drill wells or buy filtering systems. People whose communities are in need learn how to solve their water problems. Having clean water makes life better.

60

Write About Use each relative pronoun in a sentence.

1. who

_____

_____

2. whom

_____

_____

3. that

_____

_____

4. whose

_____

_____

5. which

_____

_____

Review Write a relative pronoun in each blank to complete the sentences.

1. Yesterday, I found the key _____ I had lost.

2. The girl _____ owns this bike is over there.

3. The teachers _____ classes are at recess are in the lounge.

4. Carter wears a helmet, _____ helps protect him when he is skating.

5. I asked my cousin, _____ I know can help.

UNIT 5: Adjectives and Adverbs

Adjectives and Articles

Remember   An **adjective** is a word that describes a noun. It tells what kind, how many, or which one.

The <u>yellow</u> canary flew away.   **The eagle was <u>hungry</u>.**

An **article** is a special kind of adjective. It signals that a noun will follow. There are three articles: *a, an,* and *the.* Use *a* before words that begin with a consonant sound. Use *an* before words that begin with a vowel sound.

The fly orchid looks like <u>an</u> insect. It is <u>a</u> small flower.

Think About   Look at the examples. Where does an article always come? Is that true for other adjectives, too?

_____

_____

_____

Read and Apply   Read the sentences. Circle the articles. Underline the other adjectives. Then draw an arrow from the adjective to the noun it describes.

Jade is a beautiful and rare rock. To the ancient Chinese, jade was

precious. They made sharp tools and scary masks out of it. In Egypt, jade

was a lucky stone. People still like its deep color. The shiny stone can be

white, green, or red. Today, you can find jade in an unusual necklace, a

pretty ring, or an interesting decoration.

Write About   Write a paragraph telling about a gift that you have received. Use adjectives to describe the gift and its purpose.

_____

_____

_____

_____

_____

_____

Review   Write an adjective in each blank to complete the sentences. Make sure your sentences make sense.

1. A _____ cat sat on the windowsill.

2. Luis was _____.

3. I sat on the _____ chair and read a _____ book.

4. The city is _____ and _____.

5. These _____ flowers are _____.

Comparing with Adjectives

Remember   An adjective can be used to compare nouns. For most short adjectives, suffixes are used to make the comparing forms. Sometimes the root word must be changed before adding the suffix. The **comparative** form compares two. The **superlative** form compares more than two.

	Comparative	Superlative
small →	small + er = small<u>er</u>	small + est = small<u>est</u>
happy →	happ<u>i</u> + er = happ<u>ier</u>	happ<u>i</u> + est = happ<u>iest</u>
pale →	pal + er = pal<u>er</u>	pal + est = pal<u>est</u>
mad →	mad<u>d</u> + er = ma<u>dder</u>	mad<u>d</u> + est = ma<u>ddest</u>

Think About   How can you tell if an adjective is comparative or superlative?

_____

_____

Read and Apply   Read the sentences. Find the four comparing forms that are written incorrectly. Put a line through each one and write the correct form above it.

The olderest kind of kite is a flat kite. Box kites are harder to fly

than other kites. The taller kites in the world are made in Japan. The

finnest kites are made with silk and bamboo rods. Some countries

have kite-flying competitions. The smartest kite fliers can cut down

the other kites using the kite string. After the kite is cut, people run to get

them. They go after biger and nicer kites first.

Write About

Write four sentences using comparing forms of the given adjectives. For the first two sentences, use the comparative form. For the second two sentences, use the superlative form.

Comparative

1. windy

_____

_____

2. sad

_____

_____

Superlative

3. safe

_____

_____

4. long

_____

_____

Review

Listen to each adjective. Circle **COMPARATIVE** or **SUPERLATIVE** to describe the adjective.

1.   COMPARATIVE   SUPERLATIVE

2.   COMPARATIVE   SUPERLATIVE

3.   COMPARATIVE   SUPERLATIVE

4.   COMPARATIVE   SUPERLATIVE

5.   COMPARATIVE   SUPERLATIVE

65

More Comparing with Adjectives

Remember   The comparative forms of longer adjectives are made by using the words *more* or *less* in front of the adjective. The superlative forms are made by using the words *most* or *least*.

		Comparative	Superlative
beautiful	→	<u>more</u> beautiful	<u>most</u> beautiful
serious	→	<u>less</u> serious	<u>least</u> serious

Some adjectives have special comparing forms.

		Comparative	Superlative
good	→	better	best
bad	→	worse	worst

Think About   What words are used with a longer adjective to compare two? What words are used to compare more than two?

_____

_____

_____

Read and Apply   Read the sentences. Circle the correct form of the adjective.

The French Quarter is the [most popular   popularest] spot in New Orleans, Louisiana. The [beautifulest   most beautiful] buildings in the city are found here. It is the [better   best] place to find delicious food. Many small shops and art galleries fill the street. Shoppers can find [more interesting   interestinger] treasures here than anywhere else in the city. Visitors may see the [more talented   most talented] street performers playing music here. They stop to listen to Dixieland jazz and the [less lively   least liveliest] blues jazz. There is definitely something for everyone in the French Quarter.

Write About

Write a paragraph about some place that you have visited. Use some comparative and superlative adjectives in your writing.

_____

_____

_____

_____

_____

_____

Review

Look at each sentence. Rewrite the sentence with the correct form of the underlined adjective.

1. This movie was <u>excitinger</u> than the first one.

_____

2. Cole has a <u>gooder</u> chance of winning the race than I do.

_____

3. The <u>bad</u> thing about winter is the snow.

_____

4. This display is the <u>interestingest</u> one in the museum.

_____

Order of Adjectives

Remember   Sometimes you use more than one adjective to describe a noun. Adjectives follow a specific order. They are not separated by commas.

1. Opinion 2. Size and Shape 3. Age 4. Color and Pattern 5. Origin 6. Material

I bought a <u>beautiful large new blue striped Italian leather</u> purse. [opinion, size, age, color, pattern, origin, material]

The <u>ugly old brown</u> dog sat at the door. [opinion, age, color]

A <u>tiny red glass</u> ornament hung on the tree. [size, color, material]

Think About   Why do you think there is a specific order when using more than one adjective?

_____

_____

Read and Apply   Read the sentences. Underline the groups of two or more adjectives.

Standing on the tall white English cliffs on a clear day, a person can see France across the English Channel. The White Cliffs of Dover are beautiful chalk cliffs on the coastline of England. They are England's closest point to continental Europe. Inside the cliffs are narrow dark hidden tunnels. They come from Dover Castle, a magnificent huge ancient stone castle built near the cliffs. The cliffs, the castle, and the tunnels have all played important roles in England's interesting long history.

68

Write About Write five sentences. Use the types of adjectives listed for each sentence.

1. [size, shape, color]

   _____

   _____

2. [opinion, size, age, material]

   _____

   _____

3. [shape, pattern, material]

   _____

   _____

4. [opinion, age, color, origin]

   _____

   _____

5. [age, color, pattern, material]

   _____

   _____

Review Fill in the circle next to each sentence that shows adjectives in the correct order.

O   The museum had a gorgeous small jeweled Russian egg.

O   An old silk long green beautiful scarf lay on the table.

O   The tall ancient gray stones stood 30 feet high.

O   My white furry tiny striped kitten slept on the sofa.

O   I found my brother's giant new blue rubber ball in the yard.

69

Adverbs

Remember An **adverb** is a word that describes an action word. Adverbs tell how, when, and where.

Aim <u>carefully</u> with your camera.
<u>Now</u> press the button.
Use a flash <u>indoors</u>.

Think About Look at the examples above. What does each adverb tell about the verb?

_____

_____

_____

Read and Apply Read the sentences. Underline the adverbs. Above each adverb, write _How, When,_ or _Where_ to explain what it tells about the verb.

Ansel Adams once thought he would be a musician. But he greatly

enjoyed taking photographs, too. He often traveled to wilderness areas in

America. He skillfully took pictures of mountains, rivers, and trees there.

Finally, Ansel decided to become a photographer. He strongly wanted to

protect nature. Ansel's pictures perfectly showed America's natural beauty.

Art galleries beautifully displayed his work. Today, Ansel's photographs are

still highly valued and dearly loved.

Write About Write a paragraph telling about some photographs you have taken or seen. Use adverbs to tell how, when, and where.

_____

_____

_____

_____

_____

_____

_____

_____

Review Listen to the adverbs. Circle the correct word to tell if the adverb tells **HOW, WHEN,** or **WHERE.**

1.   HOW   WHEN   WHERE

2.   HOW   WHEN   WHERE

3.   HOW   WHEN   WHERE

4.   HOW   WHEN   WHERE

5.   HOW   WHEN   WHERE

6.   HOW   WHEN   WHERE

71

Comparing with Adverbs

Remember   Adverbs can show comparison. The **comparative** form compares two actions. The **superlative** form compares more than two.

With one-syllable adverbs, add *er* for the comparative and *est* for the superlative.

Adverb	Comparative	Superlative
fast	faster	fastest
late	later	latest

For adverbs ending in *ly,* add *more* and *most* or *less* and *least.*

Adverb	Comparative	Superlative
quietly	more quietly	most quietly
slowly	less slowly	least slowly

Some adverbs have irregular comparative and superlative forms.

Adverb	Comparative	Superlative
well	better	best
badly	worse	worst

Think About   How is the comparative form made for adverbs that end in *ly?*

Read and Apply   Read the sentences. Circle the correct form of the adverb.

An okapi [closer   more closely] resembles a zebra, but it is actually related to a giraffe! Okapis were [more recently   most recently] discovered than giraffes. Since okapis hear [best   better] than many animals, they [more easily   most easily] avoid humans and predators.

Okapi males travel [more far   farther] than females to look for food. Females stand a little [taller   tallest] than the males. Okapis's tongues extend [longer   most long] than most animals' tongues. An okapi can use its tongue to clean its ears!

72

Write About   Write a sentence using the comparative or superlative form of the adverb that is given. Use a dictionary if you need help.

1. far

   _____

   _____

2. high

   _____

   _____

3. gracefully

   _____

   _____

4. badly

   _____

   _____

5. well

   _____

   _____

Review   Listen to each sentence. Circle **TWO** if the adverb compares two actions. Circle **MORE THAN TWO** if the adverb compares more than two actions.

1.   TWO   MORE THAN TWO

2.   TWO   MORE THAN TWO

3.   TWO   MORE THAN TWO

4.   TWO   MORE THAN TWO

5.   TWO   MORE THAN TWO

73

Relative Adverbs

Remember   The words *when, where,* and *why* are **relative adverbs.** They can be used to join sentences or clauses that tell about the time, the place, or the reason for something.

The house <u>where</u> I grew up is on Wood Street.

I saw Sam <u>when</u> I went out to dinner.

My fear of water is <u>why</u> I never learned to swim.

Combine the ideas in two sentences using a relative adverb.

I got home from school. I ate a snack.

I ate a snack <u>when</u> I got home from school.

Think About   What can you tell about the clause that comes after the word *when, where,* or *why?*

_____

_____

Read and Apply   Read the sentences. Underline the relative adverbs.

Tsunamis are huge ocean waves that get larger when they hit the shore. There are several reasons why tsunamis happen. Most start when an earthquake occurs in the ocean. Landslides and volcanoes erupting can also cause tsunamis. When a large amount of water is moved, a tsunami can happen.

First, large waves spread out from the place where the water moved. The waves move quickly. They get taller when the waves get close to the shore. This is why the water pulls back from the shore. A wave is usually a high wall of water when it hits the shore. Tsunamis can cause a lot of damage.

74

Write About   Read the pairs of sentences. Write a new sentence using a relative adverb to combine the two ideas.

1. The park is across the street. I play soccer in the park.

    _____

    _____

2. I visit my friend Tim. I love to play with Tim's cat.

    _____

    _____

3. I cannot eat peanuts. Peanuts make me sick.

    _____

    _____

4. Yukiko goes to the ice cream shop. She gets a milkshake.

    _____

    _____

Review   Write the relative adverb *when, where,* or *why* to complete each sentence.

1. There must be a reason _____ Mr. Davis postponed the test.

2. Thursday is the day _____ recycling is picked up.

3. Chicago, _____ my cousin lives, has a wonderful library.

4. July is the month _____ many families go on vacation.

5. Can you tell me _____ you were late for school?

6. Show me _____ your ankle hurts the most.

75

UNIT 6: Phrases, Clauses, and Complex Sentences

Prepositions and Prepositional Phrases

Remember   A **preposition** is a word that tells how things relate to each other. Prepositions go with the words that follow them. The preposition and the following words are called a **prepositional phrase.**

↓ preposition ↓
The note from Mom is on the table.
↑ prepositional ↑
phrase

Think About   Look at the example above. What does each prepositional phrase tell you about the note?

_____

_____

Read and Apply   Read the sentences. Put a line under the prepositional phrases.

Long ago, Norseman lived in northern Europe. Some days of the week are named for Norse gods. The name Wednesday comes from Woden, the king of the gods. Woden was also known by the name Odin. Thursday is named for Odin's son, Thor. Thor used his hammer to make thunder. Friday is named after Freya, the goddess of love and beauty. Freya drove a chariot pulled by two cats.

76

Write About Write a paragraph telling about your favorite day of the week. Underline prepositional phrases that you use.

_____

_____

_____

_____

_____

_____

_____

_____

_____

_____

Review Read each sentence. Circle the preposition. Then underline the prepositional phrase. One sentence has two prepositional phrases.

1. The community built a new playground in the park.

2. The girl at the front door welcomed everyone.

3. My dog dug under the fence.

4. After we arrived home, I put my coat away.

5. Police officers asked people to wait until the traffic stopped.

6. A package from my grandmother arrived today.

77

Independent and Dependent Clauses

Remember A **clause** is a group of words that act together in a sentence. A clause always has a subject and a predicate. An **independent clause** is a clause that makes sense by itself. A **dependent clause** does not make sense by itself. It needs the rest of the sentence.

Trees lose their leaves when cold weather comes.

independent clause ↑   ↑ dependent clause

Think About How can you decide if a clause is independent or dependent?

_____

_____

Read and Apply Read the sentences. Look at each underlined clause. Write **IND** above it if it is an independent clause. Write **DEP** above it if it is a dependent clause.

Starfish are not actually fish so scientists prefer the name sea star. The

most common type of sea star has five arms, but some have 10, 15, or even

50 arms. A sea star can grow another arm when it loses one. Since the sea

star's important organs are in its arms, some sea stars can even regrow

parts of their bodies.

When a sea star eats, its stomach comes out of its mouth. It forces

open a clamshell before it pushes its stomach into the shell. It pulls its

stomach back into its body after most of its food is digested.

Write About

Write a paragraph about an interesting animal. Use and label at least one independent clause and one dependent clause.

_____

_____

_____

_____

_____

_____

_____

_____

_____

_____

Review

Read each sentence. Put one line under the independent clause. Put two lines under the dependent clause.

1. Chris threw the fish back after he caught it.

2. Juanita made a phone call while she waited in line.

3. If the light is green, we can go.

4. I need a pen but I cannot find one.

5. Before Chiya left for school, she packed her lunch.

Lesson 3

Complex Sentences

Remember   A **complex sentence** is made up of an independent clause and at least one dependent clause.

One Dependent Clause   Dominic ate some cake <u>even though he was full.</u>

Two Dependent Clauses   <u>After he finished,</u> Dominic wished <u>that he had not eaten so much.</u>

Think About   What is the difference between a complex sentence and a compound sentence?

_____

_____

Read and Apply   Read the sentences. Underline the complex sentences.

Murals are large paintings. They are done on walls or ceilings of buildings. Since they are part of the building, artists try to work the style of the building into the painting. Murals have been made since ancient times, when they were often used in tombs and palaces. Murals usually show scenes that people recognize. Some artists use murals to give their opinions about current events. Other artists paint peaceful scenes because people enjoy looking at them. When a group makes a mural, the different styles can blend together.

80

Write About

Write a paragraph telling about a type of art you enjoy. Write at least two complex sentences. Underline them.

_____

_____

_____

_____

_____

_____

_____

_____

_____

_____

Review

Read the sentences. Fill in the circle next to each complex sentence.

○ If you eat that mushroom, you might get sick.

○ After 5:00, the trains are very full.

○ Marco put the glass in the sink when he was finished.

○ Amhi went for a run before she took a shower.

○ Many people have a fear of being in a closed space.

○ Mrs. Carson shut the door when she left the room.

Subject-Verb Agreement

Remember   If the simple subject of a sentence is a plural noun or pronoun, use the plain form verb for the simple predicate. If the subject is singular, use the s-form of the verb. Sometimes several words come between the simple subject and the simple predicate. Be sure the verb agrees with the simple subject.

The <u>rose</u> <u>is</u> a popular flower. <u>It</u> <u>smells</u> wonderful.

Many <u>flowers</u>, like the rose, <u>smell</u> good. <u>They</u> <u>are</u> often given as gifts.

Think About   How can you decide which form of the verb should be used in the predicate?

_____

_____

Read and Apply   Read the sentences. There are five mistakes with subject-verb agreement. Circle the five mistakes.

The Iguazu Falls is the largest waterfall system in the world. They sit on the border between Brazil and Argentina in South America. The name of the falls mean "big water." The 275 waterfalls stretches almost two miles wide. Taller than Niagara Falls, the highest fall reaches almost 270 feet. Both Argentina and Brazil protects the falls. The area around the falls is full of rare flowers and animals. Some of these is not seen anywhere else in the world.

Write About Look at the mistakes in the Read and Apply section. Rewrite these five sentences using correct subject-verb agreement.

_____

_____

_____

_____

_____

_____

_____

Review Read the sentences. Circle the correct form of the verb.

1. Our neighbors [own   owns] a dog.

2. Dad and Mom [paint   paints] the living room.

3. Dan, like many people, [enjoy   enjoys] watching football.

4. The stores at the end of the street [is   are] closed.

5. One of our cats [eat   eats] special food.

6. She [is   are] the president of the club.

83

UNIT 7: Capital Letters

Beginning a Sentence

Remember   The first word of a sentence begins with a capital letter. The pronoun *I* is always written as a capital letter, too.

> The Komodo dragon is a giant lizard.
> If I ever see one, I will tell you about it.

Think About   How do capital letters at the beginning of a sentence act as signals?

_____

_____

Read and Apply   Read the sentences. Circle each word that should begin with a capital letter.

in school, i am studying Komodo dragons. they are about ten feet long and can weigh more than 300 pounds. these lizards use their tongues for smelling. isn't that strange? you and i, of course, use our noses for smelling. the Komodo dragon eats deer and goats. this animal looks so fierce that i would hate to meet one. yet i have read that the Komodo dragon would rather hide than fight.

Write About   Write a paragraph telling about an animal that you think is scary. Use correct capitalization.

_____

_____

_____

_____

_____

_____

_____

_____

Review   Write the first word of each sentence correctly.

1. _____ Komodo dragon digs a hole for shelter.
   the

2. _____ giant lizards are found in Indonesia.
   these

3. _____ teeth are similar to shark teeth.
   their

4. _____ have seen a Komodo dragon at the zoo.
   i

5. _____ has scales and a long, forked tongue.
   it

Proper Nouns and Titles of Respect

Remember   **Proper nouns** begin with a capital letter. These include particular names of people, groups of people, places, animals, and things. In a person's name, **titles** and **initials** also start with a capital letter.

Miss Flora T. Smith   Boy Scouts of America

Morris the Cat   Oak Drive

Seattle, Washington   United States of America

Saturday   First National Bank

Think About   What kinds of words are not capitalized in a proper noun?

_____

_____

Read and Apply   Read the sentences. Circle each word that should begin with a capital letter.

One of america's greatest authors is mark twain. Mark twain's real name was samuel l. clemens. He grew up in hannibal, a city by the mississippi river. During his life, mark worked and traveled in missouri, nevada, hawaii, and europe. He wrote for newspapers and then began writing novels.

Twain heard a story while staying at angel hotel in california. Then he wrote one of his best-known short stories. It tells of the frog-jumping contest held there every year. The winners were the strongest frogs. They had names like thumper, champ, and long legs.

Write About   Write complete sentences. Use correct capitalization.

1. Tell about a place you have visited and something you saw there.

   _____

   _____

2. Tell about your favorite month and something you enjoy doing then.

   _____

   _____

3. Tell about a teacher you have had in the past.

   _____

   _____

4. Tell about a favorite pet or a special animal that you know.

   _____

   _____

Review   Rewrite these proper nouns. Use correct capitalization.

1. mr. david p. sanchez   _____

2. salt lake city, utah   _____

3. tuesday, july 19   _____

4. valley elementary school _____

5. american red cross   _____

87

Titles of Works

Remember   The first word, the last word, and each main word in a **title** of a work begin with a capital letter. This includes titles of books, stories, poems, songs, and radio or TV shows.

Book   *Tales of a Fourth Grade Nothing*
Story   "Jack and the Beanstalk"
Poem   "At the Zoo"
Song   "The Wheels on the Bus"
Show   "Elena of Avalor"

Think About   Look at the examples. When are words like *the* and *at* capitalized in a title?

_____

_____

Read and Apply   Read the sentences. Circle each word that should begin with a capital letter.

Shel Silverstein wrote songs, poems, and books. His most famous book is called *the giving tree.* He also wrote several books of poetry, including *where the sidewalk ends.* This book contains popular poems like "hug o' war," "me and my giant," and "sarah cynthia sylvia stout would not take the garbage out." Shel also wrote songs. One of his most well-known songs is called "a boy named sue." It was sung by a famous singer named Johnny Cash.

Write About   Write complete sentences to answer these questions.

1. What is the title of your favorite book?

_____

2. What is the title of your favorite TV show?

_____

3. What is the title of a song you like right now?

_____

4. What is the title of a poem that you know?

_____

Review   Read the sentences. Use the special proofreading marks to mark letters that should be capital and letters that should be lowercase.

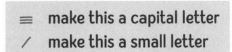

≡   make this a capital letter
/   make this a small letter

1. The campers sang "the Green grass grew all Around" by the campfire.

2. My favorite book by Dr. Suess is *the Cat In the hat.*

3. Alexa wrote a poem that she called "my sister And Me."

4. Yesterday, we watched *the peanuts movie.*

89

UNIT 8: Punctuation
End Punctuation

Remember End punctuation signals the end of a sentence. A **period (.)** ends a declarative or imperative sentence. A **question mark (?)** ends an interrogative sentence. An **exclamation point (!)** ends an exclamatory sentence or an imperative sentence that shows strong feeling.

Some trees lose their leaves in the fall.

Look at that bare oak tree.

Why don't pine trees lose their needles?

How sharp their needles are!

Be careful when you touch them!

Think About Why can two different punctuation marks end an imperative sentence?

_____

_____

Read and Apply Read the sentences. End each one with the correct punctuation mark.

Some animals have babies that look just like them Think about a puppy Doesn't it look just like a grown-up dog, only smaller

Is this true of all animals Take a look at a caterpillar Its mother was a butterfly or a moth How different these two creatures are

Do you know what a tadpole is It's a baby frog It looks like a fish until its legs grow and its tail disappears Watch out This one is almost ready to jump How much it has changed in just a few weeks

Write About   Write a paragraph about another animal whose babies look like it. Vary the kinds of sentences you use.

_____

_____

_____

_____

_____

_____

_____

_____

_____

Review   Fill in the circle next to each sentence that shows the correct end punctuation.

O Where is my hat?

O Watch out?

O The door is open.

O Look at the snow!

O Do you want a banana!

O Wash your hands.

O What time is it.

Other Uses of the Period

Remember   A **period (.)** is used after **initials** and most **abbreviations.**

Dr. S. T. Diaz   Rider Rd.
Mon.   L. Ontario

Think About   What does the period after an initial or an abbreviation signal?

_____

_____

Read and Apply   Read the sentences. Use the proofreading symbol shown below to add periods where they are needed.

⊙   insert period

The city of St Louis sits along the Mississippi R in Missouri. Pres Thomas Jefferson bought it from the French in 1803. St Louis is home of the Gateway Arch on N Fourth St The Arch is the tallest man-made monument in the country. The Eads Br is another site to see in St Louis. The bridge connects the city with East St Louis. You're in Ill after crossing the bridge.

From Apr 30 to Dec 1, 1904, St Louis hosted the World's Fair. People came from around the world to see new inventions and interesting exhibits. Famous people, including Thomas A Edison, also visited. Some of the structures from the Fair can still be seen today.

Write About

Use initials and abbreviations to give some facts about yourself. Here are some ideas: your name, your parents' names, your address, and your birthday.

_____

_____

_____

_____

_____

_____

Review

Read each group of words. Rewrite each one, using an initial or abbreviation for each underlined word. Use a dictionary if you need help.

1. 743 West Pine Avenue   _____

2. Mister Edward Jones   _____

3. Thursday, January 22   _____

4. Captain Beth Elaine Ott   _____

5. Post Office Box 999   _____

6. Lake Erie   _____

7. 5 Clipper Street, Apartment 7   _____

8. Mount Whitney   _____

Commas

Remember   A **comma (,)** is used to separate things.

- the day from the year in a date

  October 26, 2017

- the name of a city from the name of a state or country

  Memphis, Tennessee

- the name of a person being spoken to from the rest of the sentence

  What time is it, Liz?

- words like *yes, no, well,* and *however* from the rest of the sentence

  Yes, I would like a drink of water.

Think About   What signal does a comma send to a reader?

Read and Apply   Read the sentences. Use the proofreading symbol shown below to add commas where they are needed.

"Alaina are you enjoying your tennis lessons?"

    ⋀   **insert comma**

"Yes I am Kadir. I am also learning a lot about tennis. It has been around for over 100 years. The first big championship was held at Wimbledon England on July 9 1877."

"Well that's interesting. When did it come to America?"

"A woman named Mary Outerbridge brought the sport to New York City New York in 1874 Kadir. However the first American national championship was not played until September 1 1880. The first US National Championship was played in 1881 in Newport Rhode Island."

Write About   Write complete sentences using the following information.

1. Write a sentence telling today's date.

_____

2. Write a sentence telling the city or town and state where you live.

_____

3. Write a sentence addressing the person beside you.

_____

4. Write a sentence starting with the word *yes* or *no.*

_____

5. Write a sentence starting with the word *well* or *however.*

_____

Review   Write each date or city and state name correctly, using a comma.

1. February 18 2009   _____

2. Santa Fe New Mexico   _____

3. June 3 2017   _____

4. St. Petersburg Florida   _____

Write *yes, no, well, however,* or a person's name to complete each
sentence. Add commas where they belong.

5. _____ I'll bet you've never heard of a fishing cat.

6. _____ I haven't. Have you?

7. _____ I've seen them in pictures of Asia.

95

More Commas

Remember   A **comma (,)** separates three or more words used in a series. It also separates the two main parts of a compound sentence.

In a Series   Men, women, and children can become martial artists.

They can learn to kick, punch, jump, and flip.

Compound Sentences   Martial artists are calm, but they are powerful.

They practice their art, and they train very hard.

Think About   Explain where the comma goes in a compound sentence.

_____

_____

Read and Apply   Read the sentences. Add commas where they belong.

Wilma Rudolph became sick when she was young. She recovered but her left leg and foot were twisted. Doctors checked her leg talked over the problem and decided she would never be able to use it again. But Wilma's mother brothers and sisters would not give up. Every day they rubbed her leg and they helped her move it. Wilma wore a brace and she got special treatments. Before long, Wilma was walking running and even playing basketball. She eventually won Olympic gold medals in track and people called her "The Tornado."

Write About Write a paragraph about a time you did something that no one else thought you could do. Use at least two compound sentences and one series in your paragraph.

_____

_____

_____

_____

_____

_____

_____

_____

_____

_____

Review Fill in the circle next to each sentence that shows commas in the correct places.

○ You need to take out the trash, clean your room, and go to the store.

○ Raoul wants to come to the party but, he will be late.

○ Casey, Erin Luke and, Rosa went to the game.

○ Lacey will make a chocolate cake, and Stefan will decorate it.

○ The bag has paper, scissors, glue, and stickers in it.

○ Remember to water the plant or, it will die.

Apostrophes

Remember An **apostrophe (')** can take the place of the letter or letters that are left out of **contractions.** It is also used to make a noun possessive. Add an apostrophe and *s* to make a singular noun or a plural noun that does not end in *s* possessive. Add just an apostrophe to make a plural noun that ends in *s* possessive.

Contractions   we will   could not   she would   I am
                we'll   couldn't   she'd   I'm

Possessive Forms   the animal's skin   the wolves' den   the women's jobs

Think About If a noun ends in *s,* how can you tell whether it is plural or possessive?

_____

_____

Read and Apply Read the sentences. Use the proofreading mark to add apostrophes where they belong.

Wouldnt you like to know what each bird eats? Look at the beak.

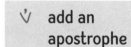
add an apostrophe

Birds beaks tell us a lot. A hummingbirds beak is long and thin so that it

can suck juice from flowers. Pelicans beaks look like pouches, dont they?

Thats so the pelican can carry a lot of fish. An eagles beak is very powerful.

The eagle uses it to catch mice and other animals.

Canaries and parakeets are often peoples pets. Canaries beaks are thick

and strong so they can crack open seeds. A parakeets beak is the same way.

Write About   Write a paragraph about some things that we get from animals. Use possessive forms of nouns and at least two contractions.

_____

_____

_____

_____

_____

_____

Review   Complete the sentences by writing the possessive form of the noun or the contraction for the words under each line.

1. _____ wool is very soft and warm.
      Sheep

2. Arguing _____ a good way to fix our problem.
          is not

3. The _____ meeting is at 7:00.
        parents

4. I found my _____ leash on the floor.
          dog

5. I _____ do that, if I were you.
    would not

Writing Quotations

Remember A **direct quotation** is the exact words a person said. Put **quotation marks** (**" "**) around the words. Use a **comma** to separate the direct quotation from conversation words like *said* or *asked.* Begin a direct quotation with a capital letter. The correct end punctuation comes before the final quotation marks. Begin a new paragraph every time the speaker changes.

Miss Harper asked, "Who was Laura Ingalls Wilder?"

"She was a famous writer," answered Emily.

Think About What do you notice about the punctuation when the conversation words come after the direct quotation?

_____

_____

Read and Apply Read the sentences. Add quotation marks and commas where they belong.

Emily said I like to read about pioneers. My favorite book is *Little House on the Prairie.* It is by Laura Ingalls Wilder.

Tony asked Why did she write about pioneers?

She was a pioneer herself. She wrote about growing up in Wisconsin, Kansas, Minnesota, and Dakota Territory replied Emily.

Miss Harper added Many settlers moved there to get free land. Then the railroad came, and even more people moved west.

It was a hard life for many families said Emily.

Miss Harper agreed Yes, they had to live off the land and start new communities.

Write About Read the conversation. Write it correctly on the lines below. Indent to start a new paragraph whenever the speaker changes. Add correct capitalization and punctuation.

Heather said my father is a harbor pilot. Enrico asked what does he do? Harbor pilots guide big ships into busy harbors explained Heather. Enrico asked is it a difficult job? Heather answered imagine trying to guide a ship through heavy traffic in a bad storm. The harbor pilot helps the ship's captain do it safely.

_____

_____

_____

_____

_____

_____

_____

_____

_____

_____

_____

_____

_____

Review Fill in the circle next to each direct quotation that is written completely correct.

○ "My new bike is blue", said Christy.

○ "Put the book on the shelf," said Ms. DiCamillo.

○ Brad asked "where is my pencil"?

○ "Jaime shouted, Go team!"

○ Marcus said, "Let's play kickball."

101

UNIT 9: Choosing the Right Word
Homophones

Remember **Homophones** are words that sound alike, but are spelled differently and have different meanings.

Their means "belonging to them." *There* means "in that place." *They're* means "they are."

Their car is over there. They're leaving now.

Your means "belonging to you." *You're* means "you are."

Look at your watch. You're late.

Two means "the number 2." *To* means "toward" or is used with verbs. *Too* means "more than enough" or "also."

At two o'clock, we plan to go to the game, too.

Think About Look at the groups of homophones above. How can you decide which homophone to use when you are writing?

_____

_____

Read and Apply Read the sentences. Circle the correct word in each set of brackets.

When [you're   your] walking along the beach, do you ever see

a cat's paw or an angel wing? [There   They're] [two   to] kinds

of seashells. A good time [to   too] look for seashells is early

in the morning. The tide washes shells onto the beach and leaves

them [their   there]. A big storm washes sea life onto the beach,

[too   two]. [Your   You're] chances of finding unusual shells is

better after a storm. Maybe, you'll be able [to   two] add some

conch shells to [your   you're] collection. [There   Their] size

and shape make them popular shells.

Write About   Use the given homophone in a sentence.

1. your

_____

2. their

_____

3. too

_____

4. you're

_____

5. they're

_____

6. there

_____

Review   Read the sentences. Cross out the incorrect homophone. Write the correct word on the line. There is one mistake in each sentence.

1. They're getting ready two leave.   _____

2. They packed there van too full.   _____

3. There is no room for you're bags.   _____

4. Maybe they need to take too cars.   _____

5. You can put your bags their.   _____

More Homophones

Remember   **Homophones** are words that sound alike, but are spelled differently and have different meanings.

Eight children ate lunch together.
We rode our bikes on the road.

Think About   How can you decide the meaning of a homophone?

_____

_____

Read and Apply   Read the sentences. Cross out the six incorrect homophones. Write the correct homophone above each one.

There are many things to see at Olympic National Park in Washington State. Many animals, like dear and bears, live in the park. Hikers enjoy trails in the mountains or along the beach. The Olympic Mountains can be dangerous. Knew climbers should not try to climb them. The Hoh Rain Forest receives from 12 to 14 feet of rain each year. You can sea interesting trees, flowers, and mosses hear. Parts of the park are on The Whale Trail, wear people can see whales from the shore. There is certainly something four everyone at Olympic National Park.

104

Write About
Look at each pair of homophones. Use each homophone in a sentence.

1. write/right

_____

_____

2. buy/by

_____

_____

3. son/sun

_____

_____

4. tail/tale

_____

_____

Review
Read each sentence. Circle the correct homophone.

1. Keira put the [flours   flowers] in a vase.

2. I tore a [hole   whole] in my jeans.

3. After we sang, Deshal [blue   blew] out his candles.

4. Mom [made   maid] two pumpkin pies.

5. If you are [board   bored], you can clean your room.

Avoiding Double Negatives

Remember   Some words mean "no." These include *no, not, nothing, none, never,* and *nobody.* Only one of these words should be used in a sentence. This is true even when the word *not* is part of a contraction.

Incorrect   There <u>weren't</u> <u>no</u> trees in the park.

Correct   There <u>weren't</u> any trees in the park.

There were <u>no</u> trees in the park.

Think About   Read the examples again. Where is the word that means *no* in these sentences?

_____

_____

Read and Apply   Read the sentences. Underline the sentences that have double negatives.

Ancient people told stories about creatures that nobody hadn't ever seen. These creatures couldn't ever be mistaken for real animals. The minotaur was half man and half bull. There wasn't nothing else like it. It was a dangerous creature, so the king built a huge maze for it. The minotaur couldn't never get out of the maze. Another creature was the sphinx. It had wings and a woman's head, but it wasn't no woman. She made people answer a riddle to pass by her. The riddles weren't never easy.

Write About   Look at the sentences you underlined in Read and Apply. Rewrite these sentences correctly. Take out every double negative.

_____

_____

_____

_____

_____

_____

_____

_____

_____

Review   Listen to each sentence. Circle **YES** if the sentence is correct. Circle **NO** if the sentence has a double negative in it.

1.   YES   NO

2.   YES   NO

3.   YES   NO

4.   YES   NO

5.   YES   NO

Misused Words

Remember   The word *good* is always an adjective. The word *well* is usually an adverb. It is an adjective only when it means "healthy."

A <u>good</u> dog obeys <u>well</u>.

The word *sit* means "to be seated." The word *set* means "to put something in a certain place."

<u>Set</u> the glasses on the table, and then <u>sit</u> in your chair.

The word *lie* means "to stretch out and rest." The word *lay* means "to put something in a certain place."

I like to <u>lay</u> a blanket on the grass and <u>lie</u> on top of it.

Think About   What kind of word does *good* always describe? What kind of word does *well* usually describe?

_____

_____

Read and Apply   Read the sentences. Circle the four words that are used incorrectly. Write the correct word above each word.

Bubbles and Bella are good friends. What is odd about that? Bubbles is

an elephant and Bella is a dog! The two live at an animal facility in South

Carolina. They play good together. Bella will set on Bubbles's back. They

will lie on the ground together. Both Bubbles and Bella are good swimmers.

They have a well time in the water. Bubbles throws a ball for Bella to fetch.

Bella brings it back and lies it down for Bubbles to throw again. After

playing and swimming, the two friends will sit together and rest.

108

Write About Write a sentence using the given word.

1. good

_____

2. well

_____

3. sit

_____

4. set

_____

5. lay

_____

6. lie

_____

Review Circle the correct word to complete each sentence.

1. My cat likes to [lie   lay] in the sun.

2. Just [sit   set] the mail on the counter.

3. Omar had a [well   good] day.

4. The teacher asked the students to [sit   set] down.

5. [Lie   Lay] the green blanket on the sofa.

6. The magician performed [well   good].

More Misused Words

Remember   The word *can* means "to be able to." The word *may* means "to be allowed to." *May* is also used to show that something is possible or likely.

I <u>can</u> climb trees. <u>May</u> I climb that one?

No, that tree <u>may</u> not be as strong as it looks.

The word *have* can be a helping verb that is used with other verbs. Never use the preposition *of* when you mean *have*.

Incorrect   We should <u>of</u> taken the train.

Correct   We should <u>have</u> taken the train.

Think About   Can you think of ways to help you remember how to use these words?

_____

_____

Read and Apply   Read the sentences. Cross out four misused words and write the correct word above each one.

There are many things we may do to help our planet. We should have

protected the plants and animals around us. Now, we can try to save some

of them. You can want to join an environmental group. You can plant trees

or raise money. You can learn about how to help endangered species.

Many extinct animals and plants could of been saved. The dodo bird

might of lived if people had not destroyed its home. Passenger pigeons could

have survived if they had not been hunted so much. People should have

been smarter. There is still time for some animals. What can you do to help?

110

Write About Write a paragraph about something you can do to help the environment.

_____

_____

_____

_____

_____

_____

_____

_____

_____

_____

Review Write _can_ or _may_ to complete each sentence.

1. _____ I borrow a pencil?

2. Miguel _____ be the best player on the team.

3. After dinner, you _____ watch TV.

4. Daisha _____ do a cartwheel.

Rewrite these sentences correctly. Replace each incorrect use of the word _of_
with _have._

5. You should of shut the window.

_____

6. We could of gone to the mall.

_____

111

UNIT 10: Writing Letters
Writing a Friendly Letter

Remember A **friendly letter** has five parts. The **heading** is the writer's address and the date on which the letter was written. The **greeting** says hello to the person who receives the letter. The **body** is the message of the letter. The **closing** says good-bye. The **signature** is the handwritten name of the writer. Use commas and capital letters correctly in a friendly letter.

Think About Why is a heading important in a letter?

_____

_____

Read and Apply Read the letter. Label the five parts of the letter.

_____ → 301 Pine Drive
                              Arcata, CA 95521
                              May 9, 2016

Dear Iris, ← _____

    What is your new home like? I wish you hadn't moved. Everyone at school misses you a lot. Do you like your new school? We are getting ready for the spring concert in band. ← _____
I am going to play soccer this summer. I hope you can come visit soon.

_____ → Your friend,

_____ → Rita

Write About Write a friendly letter to a friend or a family member. Include all five parts.

_____

_____

_____

_____

_____

_____

_____

_____

_____

_____

_____

_____

_____

_____

Review Look at the letter in Read and Apply again. Answer these questions about the letter.

1. Who is receiving the letter? _____

2. Who wrote the letter? _____

3. Where does the writer live? _____

4. When was the letter written? _____

5. Which part of the letter is indented? _____

6. What is the letter about? _____

113

Addressing an Envelope

Remember Mail a letter in an envelope. The **return address** goes in the upper left corner. This is the name and address of the person who wrote the letter. The **mailing address** goes in the middle. This is the name and address of the person who will receive the letter. A stamp goes in the upper right corner. Use commas to separate the city and state in an address. Use capital letters for proper nouns.

Return Address {
Liddy Schmidt
5 Palm Drive
Delray Beach, FL 33444

Stamp →

Mr. Jackson Brown
2390 Minnehaha Parkway } Mailing Address
Minneapolis, MN 55430

Think About Why do you think it is important to write a return address on the envelope?

_____

_____

Read and Apply Read the envelope below. Circle the letters that should be capital. Add commas where they belong.

ikuo Nguyen
38 south Hemlock ave
Nashville TN 37206

Erik perin
293 somerset rd
Somers Ny 10589

Write About

Address the envelope below. Use your own name and address for the return address. For the mailing address, write this name and address correctly: miss lylah fredericks, 2016 pendar lane, sioux falls, sd 57105. Draw a stamp in the correct place.

```
_____

_____

_____


        _____

        _____

        _____
```

Review

Look at the envelope below. Write the correct letter to show what goes in each spot. Not all the letters will be used.

```
A                                    B



                 C



D                                    E
```

1. Stamp _____

2. Return Address _____

3. Mailing Address _____

Writing a Thank-You Note

Remember   A thank-you note is a kind of friendly letter. It thanks someone for a gift or for doing something special.

> 2 Sixth St.
> Bangor, ME 04401
> July 30, 2017
>
> Dear Aunt Betty,
>
>   Thank you for letting me stay at your house for a week. I had a good time, especially when you and I hiked in the woods.
>
>   Your nephew,
>   **Brian**

Think About   What is named in a thank-you note? What is said about it?

_____

_____

Read and Apply   Read the thank-you note. Underline the gift and what is special about it. Circle the name of the person who gave the gift.

> 6248 Adams Rd.
> Baytown, TX 77520
> October 20, 2016
>
> Dear Diane,
>
>   Thank you for the book. I've wanted to read this book for a long time. It is by my favorite author. I look forward to reading it!
>
>   Your friend,
>   **Piper**

Write About Write a thank-you note to someone who has done something special for you. Write your address and today's date in the heading.

_____

_____

_____

_____

_____

_____

_____

_____

_____

_____

_____

_____

_____

Review Read the body of each thank-you note. Cross out the information that is not needed.

1. Thank you for coaching our soccer team this season. You did a great job. I wish we played at a different field. I had a lot of fun being on the team this year.

2. Thank you for new sweater. I really wanted a new pair of shoes. The sweater is my favorite color! I can't wait to wear it.

117

Grammar Handbook

Abbreviation   a short way to write a word, usually ending in a period. Abbreviations for proper nouns begin with a capital letter.

> *Examples:*   Jan.   Thurs.   Rd.

Abstract Noun   a noun that you cannot see, smell, taste, touch, or hear

> *Examples:*   friendship   loyalty   pride

Action Verb   a word that tells about doing something

> *Examples:*   grin   imagines   went

Adjective   a word that describes a noun by telling how many, what color, what size or what kind

> *Examples:*   three bikes   tiny cat

Adverb   a word that describes a verb by telling how, when, or where something happened

> *Examples:*   run slowly   play today

Apostrophe   a punctuation mark that takes the place of letters left out of a contraction or makes a possessive form

Articles   the special adjectives *a, an,* and *the*

Body   the main part of a letter

Clause   a group of words that has a subject and a predicate

Closing   the part of a letter that says good-bye

Comma   a punctuation mark that separates things or ideas

Common Noun   a word that names any person, place, animal, or thing

> *Examples:*   boy   park   cat   door

Comparative	form of an adjective or adverb that compares two
Complete Predicate	the simple predicate and all the words that tell about it
Complete Subject	the simple subject and all the words that tell about it
Compound Predicate	two predicates joined together in one sentence with the word *and*
Compound Sentence	two sentences joined together with the word *and, but,* or *or*
Compound Subject	two subjects joined together in one sentence with the word *and*
Complex Sentence	a sentence with two parts: a dependent clause and an independent clause
Contraction	two words combined into one by using an apostrophe to take the place of the letters left out

Examples:	he'll	wouldn't	can't

Conjunctions	connecting words

Examples:	and	or	but

Declarative Sentence	a sentence that tells something
Dependent Clause	part of a sentence that has a subject and a predicate but does not make sense by itself
Direct Quotation	the exact words that someone said
Exclamatory Sentence	a sentence that shows strong feeling
Exclamation Point	the punctuation mark used at the end of an exclamatory sentence
Fragment	a group of words that do not tell a complete thought
Friendly Letter	a letter written to someone the writer knows
Future Tense	form of a verb that tells about action that will happen later

119

Greeting | the part near the beginning of a letter that names the person receiving it

Heading | the part at the beginning of a letter that gives the writer's address and the date the letter was written

Helping Verb | a verb that helps a main verb tell about an action

> *Examples:* <u>has</u> arrived   <u>is</u> sleeping

Homophones | words that sound alike, but are spelled differently and have different meanings

Imperative Sentence | a sentence that asks or commands someone to do something

Independent Clause | part of a sentence with a subject and a predicate that makes sense by itself

Initial | the first letter of a name

Interrogative Sentence | a sentence that asks a question

Linking Verb | a verb that tells about being something, does not show action

> *Examples:*   is   were   are

Main Verb | the most important verb in a sentence

Mailing Address | the address a letter is being sent to

Noun | a naming word

Object Pronoun | form of a pronoun that the action is happening to

Past Participle | a special past-tense verb form used with the helping verbs *has, have,* and *had*

Past Tense | form of a verb that tells about action that already happened

120

Perfect Tense   form of a verb that uses helping verbs and the past participle of the main verb to describe action

Period   the punctuation mark used at the end of a declarative or imperative sentence and most abbreviations

Plural Noun   naming more than one person, place, animal, or thing

> *Examples:*   trees   benches   children

Possessive Noun   a noun that names who or what something belongs to

> *Examples:*   Jody's desk   dogs' bones

Possessive Pronoun   a pronoun that names who or what has something

> *Examples:*   my shoes   its tail

Predicate   the part of a sentence that tells what the subject does or is

Preposition   a word that relates the noun or pronoun that follows it to another word in the sentence

> *Examples:*   after   by   from   with

Prepositional Phrase   a preposition, the noun or pronoun that follows it, and all the words that come between them

Present Participle   a special verb form made by adding *ing* to the verb that is used with a helping verb

Present Tense   form of a verb that describes action taking place now

Progressive Tense   form of a verb phrase that uses a helping verb and the present participle of the main verb to show continuing action

Pronoun   a word that can take the place of a noun

> *Examples:*   she   he   it

Proper Noun   a word that names a special person, place, animal, or thing

> *Examples:*   Ellie   Nevada   Fido   *Mayflower*

Question Mark   the punctuation mark used at the end of an interrogative sentence

121

Quotation Marks   punctuation marks used before and after someone's exact words in a written conversation

Referent   the noun that a pronoun takes the place of

Relative Adverb   an adverb that introduces a clause that describes

> *Examples:*   where   why   when

Relative Pronoun   a pronoun that introduces a clause that describes

> *Examples:*   which   that   who

Return Address   the address from which a letter is being sent

Run-On Sentence   a group of words that tells more than one complete thought

Sentence   a group of words that tells a complete thought and makes sense

Signature   the writer's name at the end of a letter

Simple Predicate   the verb or verb phrase that tells what the subject does or is

Simple Subject   the noun or pronoun that the sentence tells about

Singular Noun   naming one person, place, animal, or thing

> *Examples:*   tree   bench   child

Subject   the part of a sentence that tells who or what the sentence is about

Subject Pronoun   form of a pronoun that appears in the subject part of a sentence

Superlative   form of an adjective or adverb that compares three or more

Title   part of a person's name or the name of a book or story

> *Examples:*   Miss Brown   Dr. Sanchez
> *Alice in Wonderland*   "Cinderella"

Verb Phrase   the main verb and any helping verbs

> *Examples:*   were laughing   are running

USING CAPITAL LETTERS

- Begin every sentence with a capital letter.
- Begin each part of a person's name with a capital letter. Include titles that are used as part of the name and initials.
- Begin words that name days, months, holidays, and places with a capital letter.

USING PUNCTUATION MARKS

End Marks

- End every sentence with a period (.), a question mark (?), or an exclamation point (!).
- End a statement or a command with a period.
- End a question with a question mark.
- End an exclamation or a command that shows strong feelings with an exclamation point.

Commas

- Use a comma before the joining word in a compound sentence.
- Use commas between words or phrases in a series.
- Use a comma between the day and year in a date.
- Use a comma between a city and state.

Apostrophe

- Use an apostrophe to show who owns or has something. If the owner is singular, add an apostrophe and *s*. If the owner is plural and ends in *s*, add just an apostrophe.
- Use an apostrophe to show where letters are missing in a contraction.

Quotation Marks

- Use quotation marks before and after a person's exact words.

Showing Titles

- Capitalize the first word, last word, and every important word in a title.
- Underline book titles.
- Use quotation marks for shorter works, such as poems and articles.

123

USING CORRECT GRAMMAR

Subject-Verb Agreement

- When you use an action verb in the present tense, add *s* or *es* to the verb if the subject is a singular noun. Do not add *s* or *es* to the verb if the subject is plural.

- If the subject is a pronoun, add *s* or *es* to the verb only if the pronoun is *he, she,* or *it.*

Subject-Verb Agreement with Forms of *Be*

- If the subject is a singular noun, use *is* for the present tense and *was* for the past tense.

- If the subject is a plural noun or compound subject, use *are* for the present tense and *were* for the past tense.

- Use the correct form of *be* with a singular or plural pronoun subject.

Present Tense		Past Tense	
Singular	**Plural**	**Singular**	**Plural**
I am	we are	I was	we were
you are	you are	you were	you were
he, she, *or* it is	they are	he, she, *or* it was	they were

124

Irregular Verbs

- The verbs below and many others are called irregular because their past-tense forms do not end in *ed*. Use the correct past-tense forms of irregular verbs.

Present	Past	Past Participle
is	was	(has) been
begin	began	(has) begun
bring	brought	(has) brought
choose	chose	(has) chosen
come	came	(has) come
fly	flew	(has) flown
go	went	(has) gone
have	had	(has) had
know	knew	(has) known
make	made	(has) made
run	ran	(has) run
say	said	(has) said
speak	spoke	(has) spoken
take	took	(has) taken
wear	wore	(has) worn
write	wrote	(has) written

Subject and Object Pronouns

- Pronouns have different subject and object forms.

- Use subject pronouns as the subject of a sentence.

- Use object pronouns after an action verb or after a preposition such as *of, to, for,* or *about.* The pronouns *you* and *it* have only one form.

Subject		Object	
Singular	**Plural**	**Singular**	**Plural**
I	we	me	us
he	they	him	them
she		her	

Naming Yourself Last

- When you speak of yourself and another person, name yourself last.

Possessive Pronouns

- Use these possessive pronouns before a noun to show ownership.

Singular	Plural
my	our
your	your
his, her, its	their

- Use these possessive pronouns when a noun does not follow.

Singular	Plural
mine	ours
yours	yours
his, hers, its	theirs

Tricky Words

- Some words are often confused. Remember to use these words correctly.

a/an	Use *a* before a consonant sound. Use *an* before a vowel sound. Wrong: **a** orange Correct: **an** orange
can/may	Use *can* to ask if or tell that you are able to do something. Use *may* to ask if or tell that something is possible or allowed. Wrong: **Can** I borrow your pen? Correct: **May** I borrow your pen?
good/well	Use *good* only as an adjective. Use *well* as an adverb unless you are describing someone's state of health. Wrong: He pitches **good.** Correct: He pitches **well.** He is a **good** pitcher. Wrong: I have a cold and don't feel **good.** Correct: I have a cold and don't feel **well.**
have/of	Use *have* or *'ve* after words such as *could, should,* and *would.* Do not use *of.* Wrong: I could **of** gone. Correct: I could **have** gone. I could**'ve** gone.
hear/here	*Hear* means "to be aware of sound": I **hear** music. *Here* means "in this place": Put your bags **here.**
its/it's	*Its* means "belonging to it": The dog wagged **its** tail. *It's* means "it is": **It's** raining.

126

lay/lie	*Lay* means "to put something in a certain place":
	She **lay** the note on the table.
	Lie means "to stretch out and rest": I **lie** down on my bed.
their/there/they're	*Their* means "belonging to them": They ate **their** dinner.
	There means "in that place": **There** you are! Sit over **there.**
	They're means "they are": **They're** the fastest runners.
to/too/two	*To* means "toward" or "for the purpose of":
	Go **to** the park **to** play.
	To can also be part of a verb form: She likes **to** skate.
	Too means "more than enough" or "also":
	I ate **too** much. You did, **too.**
	Two means "the sum of 1 + 1": The cat had **two** kittens.
who's/whose	*Who's* means "who is": **Who's** coming to the party?
	Whose is the possessive form of *who:*
	I don't know **whose** hat this is.
your/you're	*Your* means "belonging to you": Put on **your** jacket.
	You're means "you are": **You're** late for the bus.